D1408322

ANGRY MONSTER WORKBOOK
by Hennie Shore
Illustrated by Renée Williams

Published by:
The Center for Applied Psychology, Inc.
P.O. Box 61587, King of Prussia, PA 19406 U.S.A.
Tel. 1-800-962-1141

The Center for Applied Psychology, Inc., is publisher of Childswork/Childsplay, a catalog of products for mental health professionals, teachers, and parents who wish to help children with their social and emotional growth.

All rights reserved. No part of this book may be reproduced or transmitted in any form or by any means, electronic or mechanical, including photocopying, recording or by any information storage and retrieval system without written permission from the author.

© Copyright 1995 by The Center for Applied Psychology, Inc.
Printed in the United States of America.

ISBN# 1-882732-36-7

ANGRY MONSTER WORKBOOK

by Hennie Shore

Illustrated by Renée Williams

The Center for Applied Psychology, Inc.
King of Prussia, Pennsylvania

I used to be an angry kid. I'm not talking about like when something breaks and you get angry. I'm not talking about getting annoyed when my mom told me to put out the trash.

I'm talking ANGRY, with a capital "A."

I guess things got bad when I started to feel *really* mad all the time. It seemed like nobody liked me. . . not even my parents.

All they ever did was yell at me. Otherwise, they never paid any attention to me at all.

I know that I did do things to make people angry. All the time. But it was like there were these little angry monsters in my head. They were always telling me to do bad things. So I listened. . .

I was mad because my whole life seemed bad. My parents were always yelling at each other, so I stayed away from them as much as I could. I mostly hung out by myself in my room. My teachers were always telling me to try harder, but I couldn't, because I thought most of what they were teaching was dumb.

Most of the kids at school hated me because I lost my temper all the time. When someone said something I didn't like...watch out! They said I was a bully, and I guess I was, most of the time. And all the time, those monsters were talking to me, in my head. "Say that bad word!" they'd scream. "Punch that kid!" they would yell. "Break that dish! Go ahead! DO IT!"

Things were pretty bad. Luckily, though, I got some help before it was too late. My parents took me to talk to a counselor, Ms. Cole, and I talked about my feelings. I didn't like her at first, because she asked me too many questions. But it got easier as I went along, because I finally got a chance to talk.

I even told her about the monsters, though I felt embarrassed. Ms. Cole didn't act surprised at all. She even said that what I was feeling was okay, but that it was my behavior that was the problem.

She said that I had to learn to talk about my feelings more and find ways to express anger that didn't hurt or bother anyone.

When my parents talked to Ms. Cole, they learned a lot of stuff, too. They haven't been fighting as much. And they don't yell at me too much anymore.

School has gotten better, but I still think parts of it are stupid. It's funny, though...it's easier to concentrate now because I'm not so angry. And I've made some friends, too.

And those stupid monsters don't bother me too much either. I learned lots of things about being angry, so those angry monsters don't get me in trouble anymore.

Want to know how I did it? The activities in this book will show you. Maybe they'll help you tame your angry monsters, too!

I discovered that there was a lot of stuff I wanted to say. Stuff that was in my head for a long time, but I couldn't find the right words. Can you find the things I wanted to say in this word search?

I'M ANGRY	LISTEN TO ME	BE HAPPY
I HEAR YOU	TALKING HELPS	DON'T STRESS
LET'S BE FRIENDS	CALM DOWN	BE ASSERTIVE
STOP FIGHTING	I FEEL MAD	

```
C  L  L  I  H  E  A  R  Y  O  U  N  S  M  I  U
I  H  R  I  H  E  L  L  O  A  D  D  P  X  Y  B
S  D  N  E  I  R  F  E  B  S  T  E  L  F  E  E
S  T  O  P  F  I  G  H  T  I  N  G  E  A  O  A
E  S  H  A  E  O  R  S  Y  M  W  C  H  K  J  S
R  U  L  T  E  E  B  R  Z  Y  O  O  G  P  P  S
T  B  A  T  L  J  G  J  P  E  D  H  N  I  Z  E
S  I  E  J  M  N  W  P  Z  N  M  F  I  A  N  R
T  G  L  M  A  T  A  E  A  B  L  E  K  C  O  T
N  K  O  M  D  H  T  M  T  J  A  B  L  M  W  I
O  R  I  S  E  P  I  K  J  E  C  L  A  E  Z  V
D  E  N  B  F  D  L  I  S  T  E  N  T  O  M  E
```

(answers on page 63)

10

I learned to talk about what was bothering me, and find a way to feel better. Like the time I had a big fight with my mom. Can you number the pictures in order to show what happened?

(answer on page 63)

11

There were things I could do with other kids, too. Ms. Cole met with me and some other kids who had angry monsters getting them into trouble and we formed the "Tame the Monster Club." At each meeting we would do things to show that we could follow rules and cooperate. When we had a perfect meeting, everyone got points. Can you circle only the activities I did in my group?

I used to talk back to my mom all the time. "Leave me alone!" I'd say, or else I'd just ignore her. But she started to say stuff like, "I want you to get dressed for school NOW!" and she sounded like she meant it. When I would listen to her, and do what she asked, she told me how great I was. That felt really good.

But when I didn't listen, she punished me. Like once I had to use my allowance money to replace one of my little brother's toys. It broke because I threw it out the window. But it wasn't my fault. The angry monsters told me to do it. Can you connect the dots to find out how I felt?

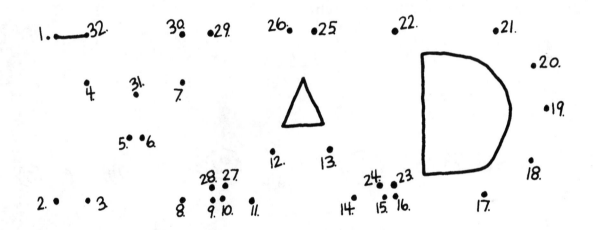

(answer on page 63)   13

I used to have a lot of fun with the kids at school, but then they said I couldn't play because I was too bossy. Ms. Cole helped me to figure out ways I could let everyone have their turn. We did some role-plays, where she was another kid, and I was "me." Then she gave me ideas for things to do instead of getting angry.

Once, we pretended that I wanted to play softball. Here's how it went:

Me: Hi. Can I play?

Ms. Cole: No, you're too bossy. We're not going to listen to you anymore.

Can you do this rebus to find out what I said?

(answer on page 63)   14

My parents and Ms. Cole came up with a behavior chart that would measure how well I was doing with anger control. If I did well for a whole week, I could get a special treat or go somewhere really neat. It was hard at first, but it got easier when I thought about my reward.

Here's a crossword of all the neat stuff I could get or do if my behavior was good.

DOWN
1 a sweet treat + "O"
2 a sucking candy
3 play with a _____
4 gift
5 potato _____

ACROSS
1 a plaything
2 go to the _____
3 toy I could dress up
4 movie treat
5 soft drink
6 video ____
7 a round toy

(answers on page 63)   15

Sometimes, after I talked with Ms. Cole, I realized how many feelings I had. Sometimes I even felt two or more at the same time, like mad, sad, and frustrated. Or, after I began to be less angry, I could feel happy, excited, and proud at the same time.

Can you think of a feeling for every letter of the alphabet? If you can think of a word for most of the letters, that's pretty good! Then pick three and tell about when you felt each of those feelings.

A   **ANGRY** _____

B _____

C _____

D _____

E _____

F _____

G _____

H _____

I _____

J _____

K _____

L _____

M _____

N _____

O _____

P _____

Q _____

R _____

S _____

T _____

U _____

V _____

W _____

X _____

Y _____

Z _____

Once I was really angry at my dad for screaming at me. I went up to my room and started throwing things—books, pillows, anything I could get my hands on. Ms. Cole told me about better physical ways to let my anger out. Eight of them are listed below.

There are eight scrambled words on this page. Unscramble them and put them in the right places.

PUNCHING _ _ _ _.   YCAL

HITTING A _ _ _ _ _ _.   LWOLIP

KNOCKING DOWN _ _ _ _ _ _.   KCSBOL

ROLE-PLAYING WITH _ _ _ _ _.   LDOSL

FINGER _ _ _ _ _ _ _ _.   GNPINTAI

PLAYING A _ _ _ _ _.   SOPTR

THROWING _ _ _ _ _.   SATDR

PLAYING AN _ _ _ _ _ _ _ _ _ _.   NIMETNUTSR

(answers on page 63)   18

Ms. Cole taught me a special way to control my anger that was named after an animal. When I felt really angry, she taught me to think about this animal going into its shell, pulling its arms and legs in tightly, closing its eyes, and hanging its head. When I did these things with my own body, I couldn't hurt or harm anyone or anything. It really helped to act like this animal.

Can you complete the picture to see which animal can help with anger control?

I never really liked to draw, and doing an art project was the last thing on my mind when I was *really* mad! But after I tried it, I discovered that drawing helped me relax and think things over.

Draw the most relaxing place you can think of in the frame below and color it in. Try to *feel* relaxed as you draw and color. When you're angry or upset, you can look at your picture. . . or draw another!

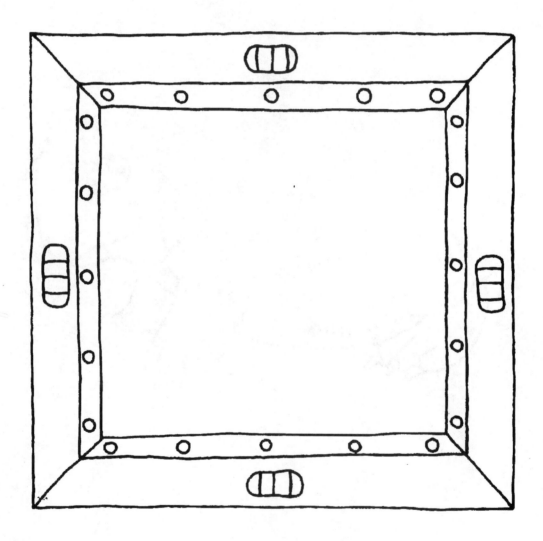

When I got angrier and angrier, nobody wanted to be with me. Ms. Cole said, "Very few people want to be around you when you have a negative attitude. Everyone likes a positive person, who talks and acts in a positive way."

Can you draw lines from the negative-thinking kid to the positive-thinking kid in each situation?

Everyone hates me.

Sue invited me to her party, but only because she had to invite everyone in the class.

Everyone thinks I'm dumb because the teacher called on me and I didn't know the answer.

I'll never be good in math.

Dad never spends any time with me. He's so busy I won't even bother asking.

This party is fun!

I can answer this one.

My dad really loves me.

Wow! I got a "B!"

I can make friends if I try.

I figured out that if I took my anger out on something that wouldn't break, then I wouldn't get in trouble for it. I'd scream at a stuffed animal, or punch a pillow, or throw soft darts at a target.

Here's a target for you, with names of people who are probably close to you. Put in on a table. Get some pebbles or pennies, and drop one at a time. Wherever your marker lands, tell about a time you were angry at that person.

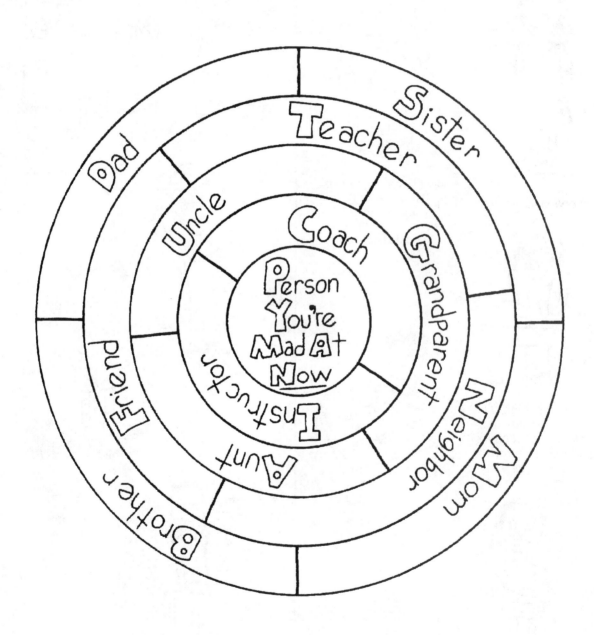

Of course, when you're angry, your temper can be terrible! I had a hard time controlling mine, but Ms. Cole told me that when I felt really mad, sometimes it helped to count to TEN and take DEEP breaths. That helped me relax.

Here's an activity to help you to remember to count to TEN and breathe DEEPly. Finish the sentences below. (Hint: Keep using TEN and DEEP)

I WAS IN A _ _ _ _ SLEEP THE NIGHT I SLEPT OUTSIDE IN A _ _ _T.

WHEN YOU HIT A BALL IN _ _ _NIS AND IT GOES PAST THE LINE, IT'S CALLED A _ _ _ _ SHOT.

I LIKE TO LIS_ _ _ TO THE SOUNDS OF THE _ _ _ _ OCEAN.

MY POCKETS WERE SO _ _ _ _, I COULDN'T FIND _ _ _ CENTS IN THEM!

I LIKE TO SWIM IN THE OCEAN, BUT OF_ _ _ THE WATER IS TOO _ _ _ _.

(answers on page 63)   23

Another trick I use to control my anger when I count to 10 is to think of something that rhymes with each number at the same time as I count. That makes me count slowly, and by the time I'm done I feel calm.

Circle the object that rhymes with each number from 1 to 10. Try thinking of each thing as you count slowly to 10, like you are running a movie in your head!

Ms. Cole helped me learn that it's okay to fight with *words*, not fists, as long as you don't hurt anybody's feelings and you really listen to the other person. She called this "fighting fair." Complete this maze and you'll learn the steps of fighting fair.

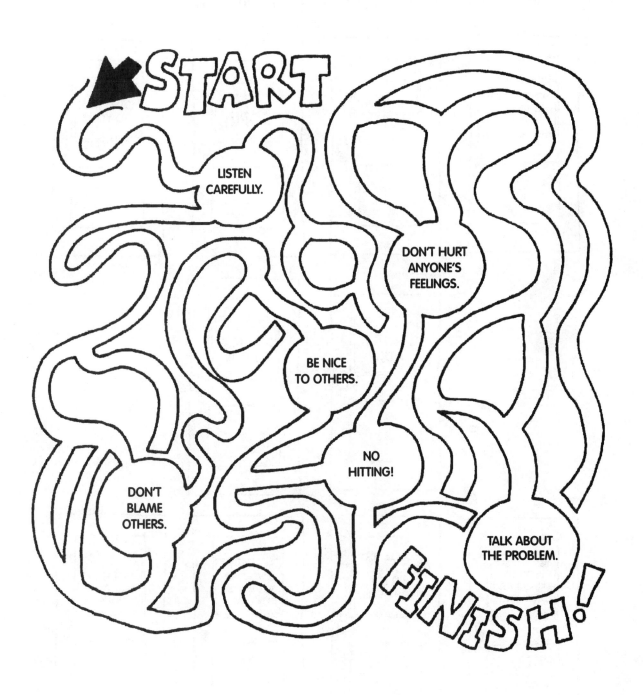

Ms. Cole said that certain things we say open the doors to understanding each other, and other things we say keep the doors shut. When the doors stay shut, you don't understand what the other person really wants or needs.

Can you "open" the doors of communication? Circle only the doors that would help people to get along better by opening communication.

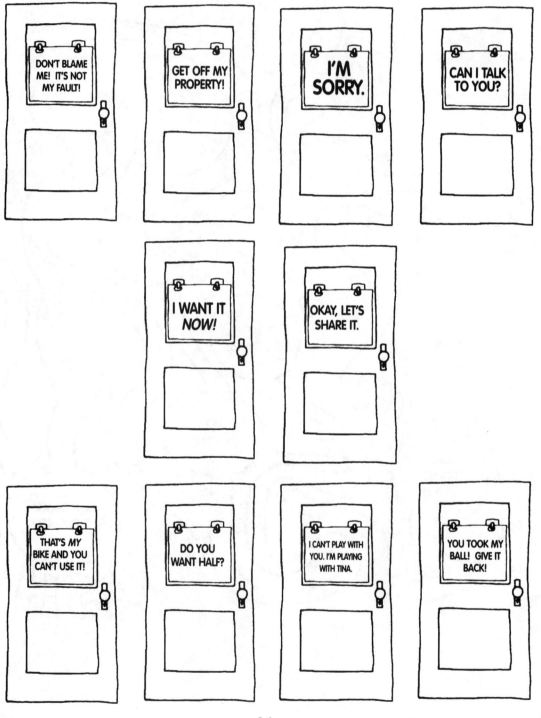

Sometimes Ms. Cole and I acted problems out with puppets. Ms. Cole said, "When we speak while thinking of someone else's point of view, we can better understand how they think or feel."

Can you make stick puppets from the family below? Cut out the figures and paste or tape a popsicle stick on the back of each one. Then act out a fight or problem that this family is having.

Now choose one person to solve the problem and come up with a good solution. Who will it be?

Some of the worst times my family and I had were when we had fights in public. One time my dad got so mad at me in a restaurant he made me sit in the car while everyone else finished eating.

Ms. Cole said that the best way to avoid fighting is to prevent arguments from happening in the first place. That takes planning. . . imagining what could go wrong and then trying to prevent it.

Suppose you went on a picnic with your family. Use this picture to help you think about all the things that could go wrong, and then list them below. How could each problem be avoided?

Problems That Could Happen   **How They Could Be Avoided**

_____   _____
_____   _____
_____   _____
_____   _____
_____   _____
_____   _____
_____   _____

Sometimes people would tell me, "Boy, you're really seeing red today, aren't you? Calm down! Get a grip!" I hated when people said that. When I was angry, I hated whenever anyone spoke to me.

But I've been thinking about that expression, "seeing red." When a person "sees red," he or she is really, really angry. Ms. Cole said that sometimes people use expressions that have colors in them to say how they feel. How many of these examples do you know?

1. IF YOU'RE HAVING A RED-LETTER DAY, IT MEANS:
a. you're feeling really sad
b. you're feeling sick
c. you're having a great day

2. IF YOU'RE FEELING IN THE PINK, IT MEANS:
a. you're feeling angry
b. you're feeling healthy
c. you're feeling tired

3. IF YOU HAVE A GREEN THUMB, YOU:
a. just played in the grass
b. can grow plants really well
c. are rich

4. IF YOU'RE FEELING BLUE, YOU:
a. are sad
b. are scared
c. are hungry

5. IF SOMEONE SAYS YOU'RE YELLOW, YOU:
a. like corn-on-the-cob
b. aren't very brave
c. have blonde hair

6. IF YOU GO AROUND WEARING ROSE-COLORED GLASSES, YOU:

a. have a good attitude

b. can't see very well

c. think everyone hates you

7. IF YOU'RE GREEN WITH ENVY, YOU:

a. don't feel well

b. are jealous

c. are friendly

8. COLOR MY WORLD MEANS:

a. be nice to me

b. leave me alone

c. talk to me

Now color in the circle below to show how you're feeling right now!

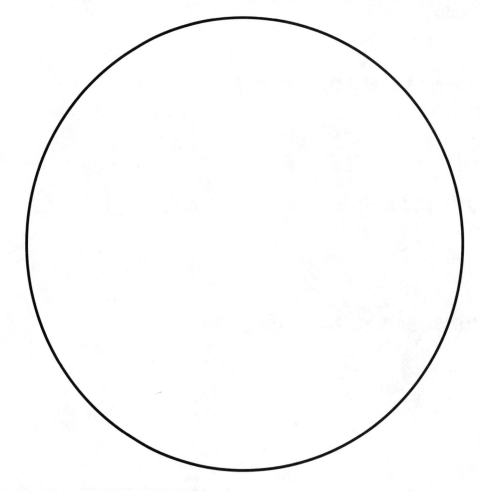

(answers on page 63)

When you're angry all the time, it's hard to make friends. I used to stay at home all the time. Mostly I just watched TV and played video games.

Then I found something that I like to do, that other kids like too. Now I invite other kids to my house to play with me. Complete the dot-to-dot to see what I'm talking about. When you're finished, you can use this page to play a popular game with a friend.

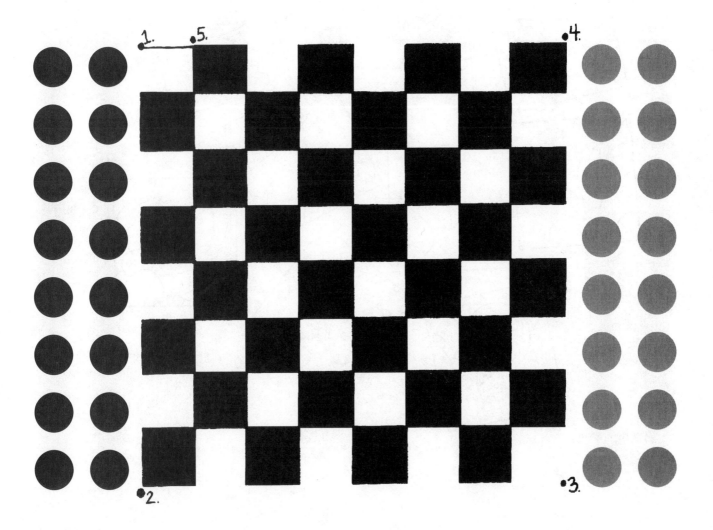

What do you like to do that other kids like too? _____

_____

Ms. Cole taught me that when I feel really mad I can close my eyes and think about a peaceful place. I use my imagination to help me calm down.

Here are puzzle pieces of a place I imagine. Make a copy of this page and cut out the pictures and put them together to see what it is.

When I was angry, nobody was ever nice to me. It seemed like nobody ever liked anything that I did.

But now people say nice things to me all the time. Can you draw lines to connect what each person (and my dog) says to me?

"That's great, honey."

"Good teamwork!"

"Nice work, son."

"That was awesome, dude!"

"Bow wow wow!"

"I always knew you could do better!"

(answers on page 63)

My mom said that I watched too many violent TV shows. She said that
violence on TV makes kids like me even angrier!

So she put me on a TV "diet." I can only watch two hours of TV a day, and no
violent shows. What shows do you watch on TV each week? Write the names
of each show below and put one "X" if it is a little violent, two "X"s if it is
pretty violent, and three "X"s if it is very violent.

MON.	TUES.	WED.	THURS.	FRI.	SAT.	SUN.

After I stopped being angry all the time, my mom and dad said that they wanted to do something "special" with me every day! They had me make a list of things I like to do, that would take about 15 to 30 minutes each, and wouldn't cost anything (or not very much). Now we pick something from my list every day and do it. (Ms. Cole calls this a "Special Time" program.)

Can you make a list of ten things that your mom or dad could do with you for 15 to 30 minutes that wouldn't cost anything (or not much)? Write it below, and then ask them if they would do a "Special Time" program with you, too!

"SPECIAL TIME" ACTIVITIES

1. _____

2. _____

3. _____

4. _____

5. _____

6. _____

7. _____

8. _____

9. _____

10. _____

Part of the reason I used to get angry was because I thought I could never be good at anything. Sports, schoolwork, reading. . . I couldn't do anything well, so I hated everything. That just made me madder, especially when I saw other kids doing that stuff with no problem.

The kid on the right is like the way I used to be, and the kid on the left is like me now. Can you find eight things that are different in both pictures? Which is the *one* thing that really helped me change?

(answers on page 64)   36

When you're angry, all you do is think about yourself. You never care how other people feel, or what they're thinking. You never even think of doing something for anyone else, just to be nice.

I learned that doing nice things for others can make you feel better about yourself. Circle the kids who are doing "good deeds," and put an "X" on those who are not.

When I was angry a lot of the time, all I did was play angry games. Can you think of a better use for the objects in each picture? Write it below each picture.

When I was little, I used to get so mad that I would hit other kids. I didn't realize how bad that was until my parents told me that I might not be able to go to school if I didn't stop doing it. They said, "Even a little kid can hurt someone very badly."

Draw a line from each kid on the left to his or her "victim" on the right.

(answers on page 64)

I hated to listen to anything anyone said, especially if they were going to lecture me about being good. I'd run away or lock myself in my room. But I was just being dumb. . . there were plenty of people who wanted to help me.

Circle the people who could give me some good advice. What would they say?

Would you be angry if someone hit you? I was, and it happened to me a lot. But I learned that I could stick up for my rights, which means that people should respect me, and the things I want, and the things I need. But only if I respect them, too. (It just makes sense!)

When my parents and I talked about rights, we agreed to respect each other as much as possible. Color only the shapes that have one dot in them to find something that will help you remember to stick up for your rights.

(answer on page 64)   41

Once I got so angry that I kicked a hole in the wall. I was really mad at the kid next door. It was his birthday, and he didn't invite me to his party. All the kids in the neighborhood were there, except me. I felt really mad, but I also felt sad too. After I kicked the wall, my parents were mad at me, too.

Write three things that I could have done instead:

1. _____

2. _____

3. _____

When I talked with Ms. Cole we talked a lot about feelings.

Here's a page full of feelings faces. Can you connect the pairs that are exactly alike? When you do, tell the feeling you think it is. Tell about a time when you felt that way.

43

Sometimes it helped me to write about what made me really angry. After I wrote stuff down on paper, I would feel better. Sometimes I could even make up with the person I was angry at.

On the scroll on the left, write a letter to someone who has made you angry. BUT DON'T SEND IT!

Now, on the right, write some things you can say to that person that will probably make the situation better.

I guess you could say that I had to jump over a lot of hurdles to learn how to tame the angry monsters. Another way to look at it is that I had to learn a lot about how to get along with others and how to calm down.

Here's a game of hurdles. Put your pencil on start. Close your eyes, and draw ten continuous arches while you leap over each of the ten hurdles. You get one point for each hurdle that you clear. You lose a point if you touch a hurdle.

Play this with a friend and see who wins. You can make copies of this page before you start, so that you can play again and again!

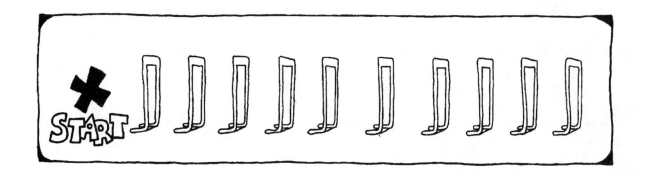

TOTAL POINTS _____

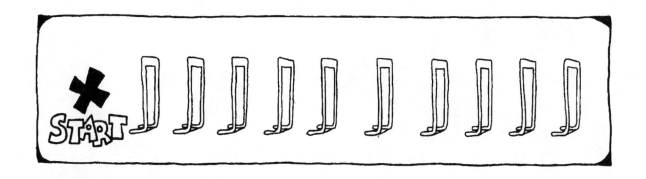

TOTAL POINTS _____

(continued)

Now list five hurdles or obstacles that you must overcome to tame your angry monsters:

1. _____

2. _____

3. _____

4. _____

5. _____

Another word for "angry" is "cross." That's why I've come up with this "cross"word puzzle for you!

To complete this puzzle, you have to fill in the blanks—in the sentences and in the boxes on the next page!

ACROSS

1. I learned to tame those _ _ _ _ _   _ _ _ _ _ _ _ _.

2. If you find yourself getting mad about something over and over again, get some _ _ _ _ _ from a grown-up.

3. One way to help yourself to calm down is to listen to _ _ _ _ _ _.

4. If you want to smash a glass, a better thing to do is _ _ _ _   _ _ _ _ _ _ _.

5. Sometimes it helps to make _ _ _ _ _ in a place where you won't bother anyone.

6. When you have angry feelings, find someone you can talk to so you can express _ _ _ _ _ _ _ _.

7. It's _ _ _ _ _ _ _ to get angry sometimes.

DOWN

1. When you are angry, people will tell you to _ _ _ _   _ _ _ _.

2. If someone makes you mad, the best thing to do is _ _ _ _   _ _   _ _ _.

3. You can express some of your angry energy if you _ _ _ _ a _ _ _ _ _ or do some other kind of activity.

4. Before you react in anger, a good thing to do is _ _ _ _ _   _ _   _ _ _.

5. When you want to relax, take deep _ _ _ _ _ _ _.

6. Use your imagination and think about a _ _ _ _ _ _ _ _ place.

7. When I have angry _ _ _ _ _ _ _ _, it helps to talk about them.

47

Ms. Cole said that when you have angry monsters in your head, making you angrier and angrier, you have to learn how to talk back to them. What would you say to each of the monsters?

WHAT WOULD YOU SAY?

I know that nobody can predict the future, but I think it's safe to say that mine looks brighter, since I learned to control my temper.

Did you ever go to a fortune teller? Here's a crystal ball, but you don't need a fortune teller to look into it. Draw your future, just the way you want it to be.

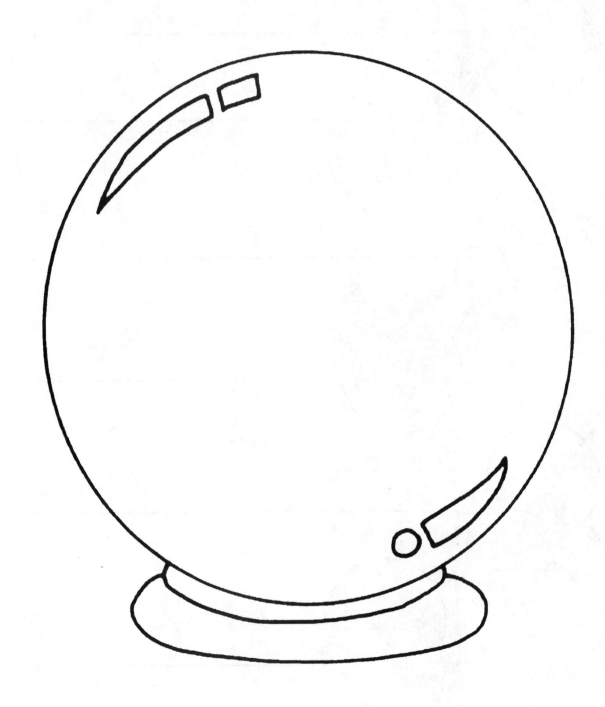

Before I tamed the angry monsters, I was always ready for a fight. I'd fight with anyone, anywhere, any time.

These kids are ready to fight. They're really mad at each other! To avoid fighting, they need to hold something. Find the six shaded objects in this picture, and then use the first letter of each object to find out what they should hold.

THEY NEED TO HOLD THEIR __ __ __ __ __ __**S.**

(answers on page 64)   51

It used to be that whenever I got teased, I'd explode! Now kids don't tease me as much, because I've learned how to get along better with them.

Here's an activity that uses a different kind of "Ts." Tom had a big problem with anger. If you can complete this phrase by figuring out all the words that begin with "T," you'll be giving him some good advice.

T__ __ __
(opposite of "give")

T__ __ __
(what a clock tells)

T__
(homonym of "two")

T__ __ __
(a cat is this, a lion isn't)

T__ __ __'s
(the person in this statement)

T__ __ __ __ __ .
(what you lose when you're angry)

(answers on page 64)   **52**

My parents were always trying to get me to make friends. But I thought the other kids were geeks, and besides, they didn't like me either. It was hard to learn how to make friends, but I did it.

Here are some cryptograms that will help you to make friends if you say them to yourself. (The numbers correspond to the letters of the alphabet).

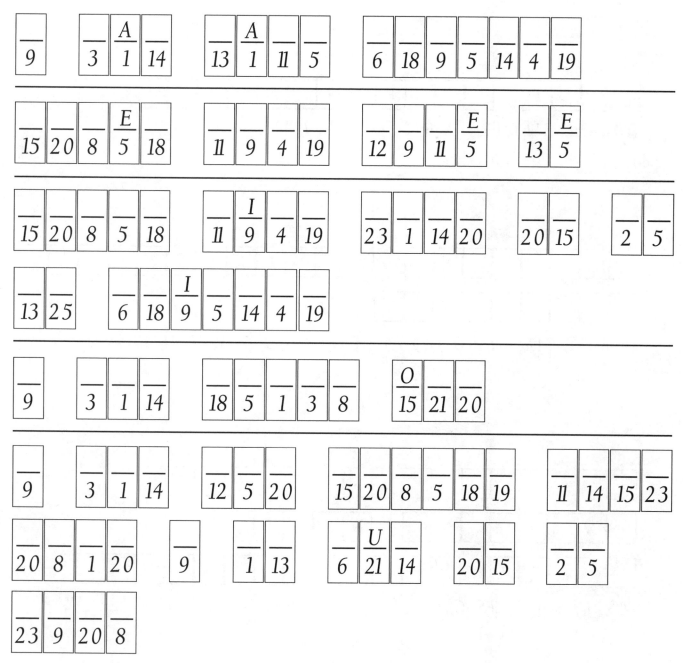

(answers on page 64)

There's a TV show where you guess the word, or name, or phrase. On the show, they fill in the letters R, S, T, L, N, and E, so I did too. Fill in the missing letters to complete each well-known phrase about fighting.

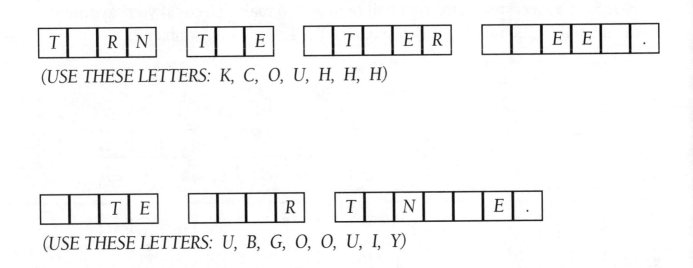

| T | | R | N | | T | | E | | | T | | E | R | | | E | E | | . |

(USE THESE LETTERS: K, C, O, U, H, H, H)

| | T | E | | | | R | | T | | N | | E | . |

(USE THESE LETTERS: U, B, G, O, O, U, I, Y)

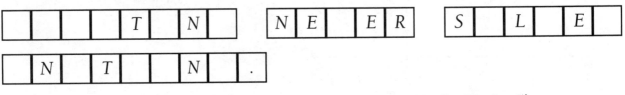

| | | | T | | N | | | N | E | | E | R | | S | | L | | E | |
| | N | | T | | | N | | . |

(USE THESE LETTERS: D, G, F, A, V, O, H, I, I, Y, V, G, H, I, G)

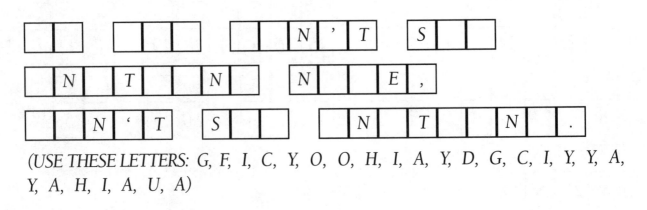

							N	'	T		S		
	N		T		N		N		E	,
	N	'	T		S				N		T		N		.

(USE THESE LETTERS: G, F, I, C, Y, O, O, H, I, A, Y, D, G, C, I, Y, Y, A, Y, A, H, I, A, U, A)

(answers on page 64)   **54**

When people say, "That really bugs me," they are saying, "That really annoys me," or "That really makes me angry."

Here's a whole page for you to draw in things that really "bug" you. Circle the things or situations that you can make better.

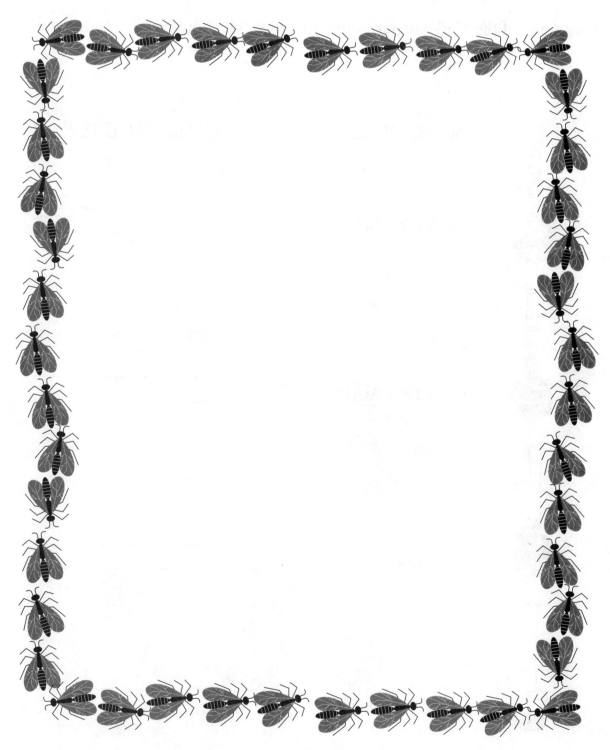

Ms. Cole explained that everyone gets mad once in a while, but only *really* angry people (like I used to be) get *boiling mad*—a lot.

The mercury in this Mad-o-meter goes higher as a person gets frustrated, then mad, then furious, then to the "boiling point."

Choose one of the Mad-o-meter points that best tells how you feel today and write in why you feel that way.

<u>MAD-O-METER</u>   <u>WHY DO YOU FEEL THIS WAY?</u>

BOILING MAD   _____
                     _____

FURIOUSLY MAD   _____
                     _____

MAD   _____
                     _____

FRUSTRATED   _____
                     _____

I had a big problem with controlling my temper. Every time someone said something that I thought was mean, I'd have a tantrum.

With Ms. Cole's help, I learned to calm down and tame my temper. One way I did this was to think of the angry monsters as tame and furry animals.

Draw your version of how an angry monster would look if it was tame and furry.

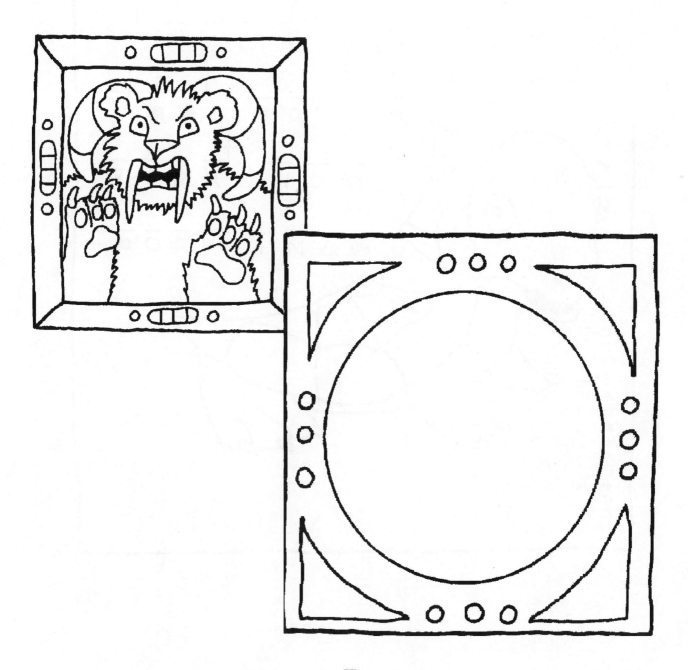

57

I also learned the "turtle technique" of controlling your anger. I would act like a turtle and go into my "shell" instead of acting in an angry way. This gave me a chance to think about things before I acted.

Temper Turtle is asking you to do something that will help you understand your anger. Figure out what he is saying and then follow his directions.

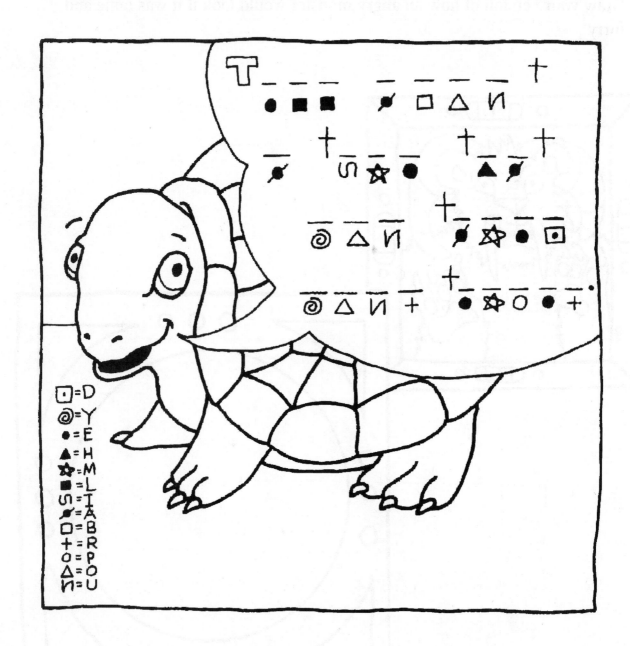

(answer on page 64)

One of the things I did with Ms. Cole was tell stories. One of us would start a story, and then the other would finish it. She said this helped both of us work on my anger problem.

Here's the beginning of a story about an angry kid. Can you write two or three (or more) sentences to finish it?

> Once there was an angry kid named
> Joe. He was having a very bad day
> because his parents woke him up
> with their first fight of the day...

Everyone wanted me to behave better, but I just said, "Why should I?" Ms. Cole made me understand that if everyone did exactly what they wanted to do all the time, the world would be a pretty bad place.

Here's a playground scene with "good" and "bad" kids. Circle the ones who are doing things they shouldn't be doing, and tell why you think they are "bad" things.

Ms. Cole had this big poster that had a traffic light on it, just like the one below. It was to help kids like me remember to stop, think, and then proceed (or go). To the right of each part of the traffic light, write about a time when you got angry, then thought about what would happen if you took your anger out on someone or something, and then what you did to overcome your anger.

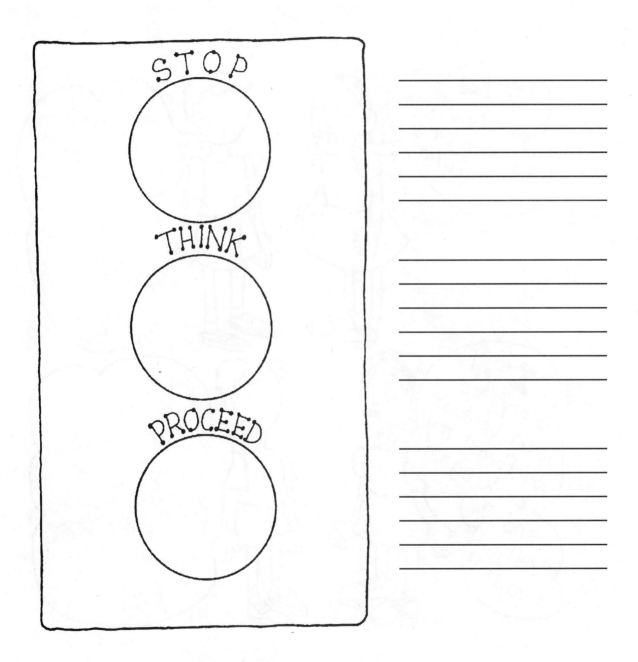

I never thought about how others felt when I got angry at them. But now I do, and I try to stop and think about how I should act before I do something. Here are two ways that the girl on the left could tell the boy on the right that she's angry at him. Tell what you think the boy would say, and draw in his face showing how he would feel.

PAGE 10 -

```
C L L  I H E A R Y O U  N S M I U
I H R I H E L L O A D D P X Y B
S D N E I R F E B S T E L F E E
S T O P F I G H T I N G E A O A
E S H A E O R S Y M W C H K J S
R U L T E E B R Z Y O O G P P S
T B A T L J G J P E D H N I Z E
S I E J M N W P Z N M F I A N R
T G L M A T A E A B L E K C O T
N K O M D H T M T J A B L M W I
O R I S E P I K J E C L A E Z V
D E N B F D L I S T E N T O M E
```

PAGE 11 -

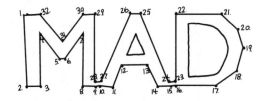

PAGE 13 -

PAGE 14 - That's OK. I will do what you want to do. Then maybe we can do what I want to do.

PAGE 15 -

PAGE 18 - punching clay, hitting a pillow, knocking down blocks, role-playing with dolls, finger painting, playing a sport, throwing darts, playing an instrument

PAGE 19 - turtle

PAGE 23 - I was in a deep sleep the night I slept outside in a tent.
When you hit a ball in tennis and it goes past the line, it's called a deep shot.
I like to listen to the sounds of the deep ocean.
My pockets were so deep, I couldn't find ten cents in them!
I like to swim in the ocean, but often the water is too deep.

PAGE 24 - 1. sun 2. shoe 3. tree 4. door
5. hive 6. sticks 7. heaven 8. plate 9. line
10. pen

PAGE 30 - 1.-c 2.-b 3.-b 4.-a 5.-b 6.-a
7.-b 8.-a

PAGE 33 -
Mother: "That's great, honey!"
Father: "Nice work, son!"
Teacher: "I always knew you could do better!"
Dog: "Bow wow wow!"
Friend: "That was awesome, dude!"
Coach: "Good teamwork!"

PAGE 36 - hats, hair, shirts, wristbands, star on shorts, socks, shoes, boy/girl

PAGE 39 -
hitting - kid with eye patch
pushing - kid on ground crying
throwing an object - kid with bandage on arm
biting - kid with swelled finger
tripping - kid holding knee
kicking - kid with welt on leg

PAGE 41 - "R"

PAGE 48 -

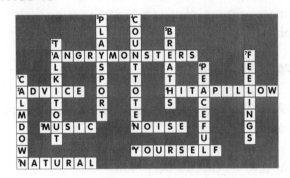

PAGE 51 - They need to hold their tempers.

PAGE 52 - Take Time To Tame Tom's Temper

PAGE 53 -
I can make friends.
Other kids like me.
Other kids want to be my friends.
I can reach out.
I can let others know that I am fun to be with.

PAGE 54 -
Turn the other cheek.
Bite your tongue.
Fighting never solved anything.
If you can't say anything nice, don't say anything.

PAGE 58 - Tell about a time that you tamed your temper.